HAL•LEONARD
INSTRUMENTAL
PLAY-ALONG

AUDIO
ACCESS
INCLUDED

VIOLA

JAMES BOND

T0070696

PLAYBACK+
Speed • Pitch • Balance • Loop

To access audio visit:
www.halleonard.com/mylibrary

Enter Code
5170-9418-9166-8420

Audio arrangements by Peter Deneff

ISBN 978-1-4950-6086-1

Music Sales America

EXCLUSIVELY DISTRIBUTED BY

HAL•LEONARD®

7777 W. BLUEMOUND RD. P.O. BOX 13819 MILWAUKEE, WI 53213

Visit Hal Leonard Online at
www.halleonard.com

TITLE	PAGE

DIAMONDS ARE FOREVER

from DIAMONDS ARE FOREVER

Words by DON BLACK
Music by JOHN BARRY

VIOLA

FOR YOUR EYES ONLY

from FOR YOUR EYES ONLY

VIOLA

Lyrics by MICHAEL LESSON
Music by BILL CONTI

FROM RUSSIA WITH LOVE

from FROM RUSSIA WITH LOVE

VIOLA

Words and Music by
LIONEL BART

GOLDFINGER
from GOLDFINGER

VIOLA

Music by JOHN BARRY
Lyrics by LESLIE BRICUSSE and ANTHONY NEWLEY

JAMES BOND THEME

VIOLA

By MONTY NORMAN

LIVE AND LET DIE
from LIVE AND LET DIE

VIOLA

Words and Music by PAUL McCARTNEY
and LINDA McCARTNEY

NOBODY DOES IT BETTER

from THE SPY WHO LOVED ME

VIOLA

Music by MARVIN HAMLISCH
Lyrics by CAROLE BAYER SAGER

ON HER MAJESTY'S SECRET SERVICE - THEME

VIOLA

By JOHN BARRY

SKYFALL
from the Motion Picture SKYFALL

VIOLA

Words and Music by ADELE ADKINS
and PAUL EPWORTH

A VIEW TO A KILL
from A VIEW TO A KILL

VIOLA

Words and Music by JOHN BARRY
and DURAN DURAN

WRITING'S ON THE WALL

from the film SPECTRE

VIOLA

Words and Music by SAM SMITH
and JAMES NAPIER

YOU ONLY LIVE TWICE

from YOU ONLY LIVE TWICE

VIOLA

Music by JOHN BARRY
Lyrics by LESLIE BRICUSSE